THE PICTURE LIFE OF
MIKHAIL GORBACHEV

THE PICTURE LIFE OF
MIKHAIL GORBACHEV

BY JANET CAULKINS

FRANKLIN WATTS
NEW YORK/LONDON/TORONTO/SYDNEY/1985

Frontispiece: winter night on Red Square
facing the Kremlin wall. The low building
in front of the wall is Lenin's tomb.

"Mad hatter of Red Square" headline published March 27, 1985,
reprinted by permission of New York Post copyright 1985 NGP.

Map by Vantage Art.

Cover photograph courtesy of Sovfoto.

Photographs courtesy of Paolo Koch/Rapho/Photo Researchers, Inc.:
frontispiece; AP/Wide World: pp. 6, 14, 18, 37; UPI/Bettmann Newsphotos:
p. 9; Sygma: pp. 10, 33, 34; Robert Capa/Magnum Photos, Inc.: p. 13;
Novosti from Sovfoto: p. 17; Tass from Sovfoto: pp. 21, 25, 29 (top),
30 (top), 41 (top); Photoreporters, Inc.: p. 22; 1980 Burt Glinn/
Magnum Photos, Inc.: p. 29 (bottom); Fabian/Sygma: p. 30 (bottom);
Matthew Ford/Photoreporters, Inc.: p. 38; Dave Valdez/The White House:
p. 41 (bottom); Marc Riboud/Magnum Photos, Inc.: p. 42.

Library of Congress Cataloging in Publication Data

Caulkins, Janet Hillier.
The picture life of Mikhail Gorbachev.

Includes index.
Summary: An illustrated biography of the new
leader of the Soviet Union including a chronology of
important dates in his life and a glossary of Soviet
political words.
1. Gorbachev, Mikhail Sergeyevich, 1931-   —Portraits,
caricatures, etc.—Juvenile literature.
2. Heads of state—Soviet Union/Biography—Juvenile
literature. [1. Gorbachev, Mikhail Sergeyevich,
1931- . 2. Heads of state] I. Title.
DK290.3.G67C38 1985   947.085'4'0924 [92]   85-15023
ISBN 0-531-10085-5

CONTENTS

A NEW LEADER

It is a solemn moment. Red and black flags
are blowing in the cold wind that sweeps
over Red Square in Moscow. Thousands of
soldiers in high boots and heavy fur hats
stand in the snow, as the open coffin of
Konstantin Chernenko is carried slowly past
them, to the mournful music of Chopin's
Funeral March.

Leading the mourners who walk behind
the coffin is the new leader of the largest
nation in the world, the Soviet Union. It is
Mikhail S. Gorbachev.

Mikhail Gorbachev and Foreign
Minister Andrei Gromyko follow
the open coffin of Konstantin
Chernenko in Red Square.

All the nations of the world are eager to know about the new Soviet leader. The Soviet Union is huge—more than twice as big as the United States—and it is the second strongest industrial country in the world.

The United States is particularly concerned. During World War II, the Soviets were our allies, but relations between us have been tense and unfriendly for the last forty years. In the 1950s and 1960s, the two nations were so hostile the situation was known as the *Cold War*.

This is Nikita Khrushchev, who was the Soviet leader in the days of the Cold War. Here he is angrily addressing the U.N. General Assembly. At one point he even took off his shoe and banged it on the desk.

Now we want to know what the new Soviet leader is like. Will his government be even more hostile to the United States? Or will he be flexible, ready to join in the "give-and-take" that has to exist among nations that want to get along together?

It is too soon to tell, but we do know that Mr. Gorbachev (pronounced gore-bah-CHAWFF) is different in many ways from earlier Soviet leaders.

He is young, well educated, interested in new ideas, and impatient with red tape. But he is also part of the Soviet one-party system. In his own words he is eager to "enhance the influence of socialism in world affairs."

This informal picture of Mikhail Gorbachev shows a birthmark on his head. "Official" photographs are sometimes retouched to conceal it.

UP FROM THE RANKS

Mikhail Gorbachev was born on March 2, 1931, in the village of Privolnoye near Stavropol in the northern Caucasus. His parents were peasants. They were very poor.

A peasant family
in prewar Soviet Union.
Notice the thatched roof.

Mikhail was eight years old when World War II began. The invading German army occupied Stavropol, and the fighting left the countryside in ruins.

The German occupation of his homeland made a deep impression on Mikhail, as it did on all Russians. War destruction was more terrible there than in any country; 20 million Russian lives had been lost by the time the war ended.

After the war teenage Mikhail spent school vacations laboring in the wheat fields. He drove an old-fashioned combine harvester that had no cab. Late in the harvest season the weather was bitterly cold, and Mikhail wrapped straw around himself to keep warm.

One of the villages destroyed in
World War II. The German army burned
the houses and the farm equipment
and carried off all the grain and cattle.

As a young man in Stavropol, Mikhail worked as an organizer with the Communist Youth League, the *Komsomol*.

This was of importance to his future. In the USSR there is only one party—the *Communist Party of the Soviet Union (CPSU).* Anyone who rises to high political office must be a member. Membership is on a trial basis. You must prove your loyalty and interest before you are accepted. It was through the Komsomol that Gorbachev got his political start.

Members of the Komsomol, the Communist Youth League. This is an important organization, which is viewed as the training ground for the nation's future leaders.

When he was nineteen, Mikhail had a stroke of luck. He was accepted at the law school of Moscow State University, the finest university in the Soviet Union. His work with the Komsomol probably helped.

After he graduated, Mikhail went back to Stavropol. He became an official of the city Komsomol, a job that would lead to quick promotion. He also took some special courses and earned another degree— this time in agricultural economics.

Moscow University is an immense building. It is the Soviet Union's showplace of higher education.

Mikhail was interested in improving conditions for farmers and workers. He never forgot those cold days working in the wheat fields. A career in politics seemed the best way to make these improvements, and Mikhail moved up steadily through the ranks of the Communist party.

At the age of 47, Gorbachev became secretary for agriculture in the *Central Committee* of the Communist Party. This is a very important position. The USSR has a brief, often harsh, growing season. Most of the Soviet Union is in the same latitude as Northern Canada and Alaska, and there is a huge population to feed.

Only 10 percent of the land is arable. Despite its size, the USSR cannot grow enough crops to feed its people.

Gorbachev met his wife, Raisa Maksimovna, while he was taking evening courses back in Stavropol. She was then a primary school teacher. Mikhail and Raisa had a little girl and named her Irina. Irina is now in her twenties. She is a physician, is married to a doctor and has a daughter, Oksana.

Because of Gorbachev's new job, the family moved to Moscow. Raisa studied at the University, where she now teaches philosophy.

Gorbachev was good at his job. He cut through red tape and got things done, and he was able to do it without getting people upset. He was smart and full of energy. Devotion to the Party added to his success, and by 1980 he was a very important man in Soviet politics.

Raisa Gorbachev

FACING THE CHALLENGE

Today Mikhail Gorbachev is the head of the Soviet Communist Party and the new leader of the Soviet Union. These days his five-year-old granddaughter, Oksana, says she doesn't see enough of him because he works too hard.

To understand what is so hard about Mr. Gorbachev's job, we should look at a few facts about the USSR.

USSR stands for Union of Soviet Socialist Republics. This huge country is made up of fifteen nations, or soviets, and covers one-seventh of the land area of the earth.

Chess players in Moscow

SOVIET SOCIALIST REPUBLICS

Lena R.

Angara R.

Amur R.

China

Mongolia

Although we often speak of the Soviet Union as Russia, that is not really correct. Russia is *in* the Soviet Union. It is the largest, most powerful of the Soviet Republics—almost twice the size of the United States—and Russian is the official language of the USSR.

But the Soviet Union includes over 100 different ethnic groups speaking many different languages. They live in climates from Arctic cold to tropical heat, and from mountain ranges covered with thick forests to arid deserts where camels are used for transportation.

The customs of these nations, and the way their people dress and live are often centuries apart.

A shepherd and
his family in
Kirghizian SSR

Shepherds with
camels in desert
of Turkmenian SSR

There are Muslim villages in Central Asian USSR, and European-style cities on the western borders. There are nomads who roam in the frozen north and Turkish tribes that survive in the harsh deserts.

Forests cover 40 percent of the USSR, and only 10 percent of the land is good for farming.

All these nationalities, with their different needs and interests, are governed and controlled by the *Secretariat* and the *Politburo* of the Communist Party.

Now Mikhail Gorbachev is the man in charge and he has a very big job!

Top: a view of Moscow at night

Bottom: a section of the Trans-Siberian gas pipeline, one of the world's most impressive construction projects

A DIFFERENT KIND
OF SOVIET LEADER?

Mikhail Gorbachev is the youngest person ever to lead the Soviet state—nineteen years younger than Chernenko, the last leader, and twenty years younger than our own president.

Whereas the two leaders before him were old men in poor health, Gorbachev is very active and health-conscious. He takes long walks, doesn't smoke, and drinks only moderately.

And unlike the leaders before him, Mr. Gorbachev has traveled widely, in the West as well as in eastern Europe. He has had a chance to see what life is really like in other parts of the world.

Gorbachev toured an industrial meat-packing
plant in Canada in 1983. His curiosity
and eagerness to learn from "outsiders"
is very unusual among Soviet leaders.

Mad hatter of Red Square

When he visited Canada, Mr. Gorbachev was good tempered and patient. He even clowned for photographers.

But he had a serious purpose. He visited factories and farms, and he asked the workers about their families and their way of life; he especially wanted to know how and why workers there produced so much more than Soviet workers.

The many hats of Mr. Gorbachev, as he clowns for the Canadian press.
Top: holding a giant bologna.
Bottom left: at a ketchup factory.
Bottom right: at a Canadian barbecue.

Perhaps Gorbachev will try to make a few changes in the rigid system at home, so Soviet workers will want to work harder and produce more.

One thing we may be sure Gorbachev will not try to change is the voting system. He believes very strongly in the Communist Party, which runs the country.

In the Soviet one-party system, the candidates are all chosen by the Communist Party. There is no choice of candidates such as we have, and there is no *secret ballot.* You vote "for" by dropping an unmarked ballot in the box. To vote "against," you must open the ballot and cross off the name you wish to vote against.

Granddaughter "Ksanochka" (a pet name for Oksana) comes along to watch her grandfather vote in Parliamentary elections in Moscow.

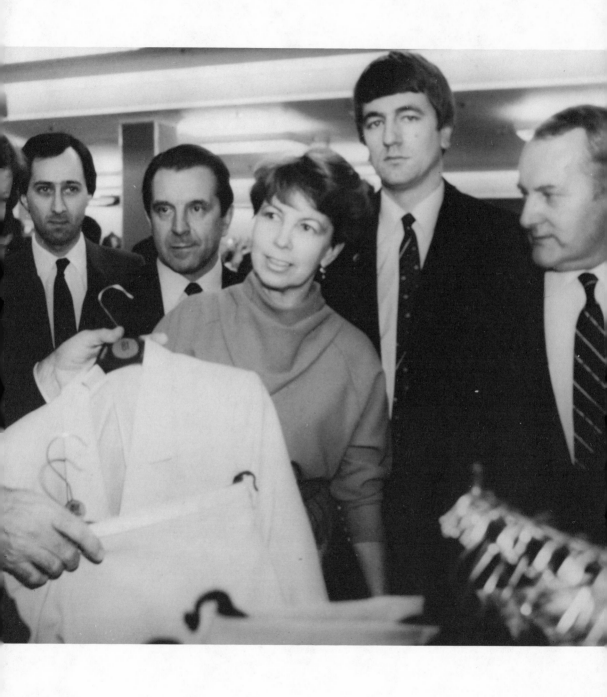

Mikhail and Raisa Gorbachev visited England in 1984. They surprised everyone there with their charm, humor, and outgoing ways.

Raisa was slim and fashionable. She wore elegant clothes and talked about her interest in English literature and culture. She made many of her own plans about things to do and places to see.

On the Gorbachev's London visit, Raisa decided on her own to visit a London department store. This, too, is most unusual for the wife of a Soviet official.

Mr. Gorbachev talked easily and informally to all kinds of people. He even addressed a committee of the British Parliament. He talked about the need for peace and disarmament.

This was not the style westerners expect from Soviet leaders. The British press took to calling him "Mr. G." Margaret Thatcher, the British prime minister said "I like Mr. Gorbachev; we can do business together."

When Gorbachev became the new leader of the Soviet Union, President Reagan sent a letter inviting him to visit the United States. We don't expect to see any big changes in Soviet politics, but perhaps we, too, will find that we can "do business together."

Top: Mr. Gorbachev and Margaret Thatcher, the British prime minister
Bottom: George Bush, vice president of the United States, meeting with Mr. Gorbachev in Moscow

IMPORTANT DATES IN THE LIFE OF MIKHAIL S. GORBACHEV

1931	Born March 2, in village of Privolnoye in Stavropol region.
1942	German army occupies Stavropol (then called Voroshilovsk).
1940s	After the war, as a teenager, Gorbachev works at a local machine tractor station during school vacations. Becomes member of the Komsomol (Communist Youth League).
1950	Enrolls in law school of Moscow State University.
1952	Joins the Communist Party.
1955	Graduates from the University of Moscow with a law degree.

Moscow's Red Square. The Kremlin, the
seat of Russian government, is to the right.

1950s and 60s	Returns to Stavropol and continues his career in the party organization. Takes correspondence and evening courses in agronomy. Meets and marries Raisa Maksimovna. Daughter Irina is born.
1967	Receives his degree in agricultural economics.
1970	Named first secretary of the regional organization (Stavropol Province) of the Communist Party.
1971	Joins the Central Committee.
1974	Elected chairman of the Youth Affairs Commission of the Supreme Soviet.
1970s	Heads delegations to Belgium and West Germany.
1978	Called to Moscow as party secretary for agriculture in the Central Committee.
1979	Becomes candidate member of Politburo.
1980	Becomes full member of Politburo.
1981	Awarded the Order of Lenin "for great services to the party and the State."

1982   Soviet President Leonid Brezhnev
        dies at age 76. Yuri Andropov, 68,
        named as Brezhnev's successor.

1983   Death of Yuri Andropov. Konstantin
        Chernenko, 72, named as new
        general secretary and president of
        the Soviet Union.
        Gorbachev heads delegation on a
        visit to Canada. Appears before the
        standing committee of the House
        of Commons and the Senate on
        external affairs and national defense.

1984   Visits Great Britain and appears
        before Parliament's foreign relations
        committee.

1985   Death of Konstantin Chernenko.
        Gorbachev, 54, named as new
        general secretary of the Communist
        Party and leader of the Soviet Union.
        Andrei A. Gromyko named president of the
        Soviet Union at the request of Gorbachev.

GLOSSARY OF POLITICAL WORDS

Central Committee (of the Communist Party):
Several hundred members, chosen from
people elected by Communist Party
organizations across the country. The
Central Committee elects the members of
the Politburo and the Secretariat.

Cold War: "The Cold War," capitalized,
refers to the hostility and mistrust between
the Soviet Union and the Western nations,
especially during the 1950s and 1960s. A
"cold war," without capitals, means any
hostile activity or long-lasting tension among
nations, without actual war.

Communist Party of the Soviet Union (CPSU):
The party that governs the Soviet Union. There
is no other political party. To join the CPSU,
a person must be recommended by other
members. Then he or she must spend a year
on probation before being officially accepted.

General Secretary: The most powerful
person within the Communist Party. The
General Secretary is chairman of the
Politburo and the Secretariat. Mikhail
Gorbachev is now the General Secretary.

Komsomol: The Communist Youth League. The most important youth organization, for ages fourteen to twenty-four years. It is set up and closely controlled by the Communist Party.

Politburo: The most powerful group in the Communist Party. It sets the overall policy for the Soviet Union.

Secret ballot: A way to be sure there is free choice in voting. The voter's choice is kept private to protect the voter from outside interference.

Secretariat: One of the two top groups in the Communist Party of the Soviet Union (the other is the Politburo). The Secretariat is in charge of the day-to-day affairs of the Soviet Union. Together, the Secretariat and the Politburo run the country.

Supreme Soviet: The Soviet parliament elected by all Soviet citizens over eighteen. All candidates are approved by the Communist Party, and there is only one candidate for each position.

INDEX